# Peace
## AND
# Goodwill

RACHEL QUILLIN

*For* unto you is born this day in the city of David a Saviour, which is Christ the Lord.

And this shall be a sign unto you; Ye shall find the babe wrapped in swaddling clothes, lying in a manger.

And suddenly there was with the angel a multitude of the heavenly host praising God, and saying,

Glory to God in the highest, and on earth peace, good will toward men.

LUKE 2:11–14

# The Prince of Peace

For unto us a child is born, unto us a son is given:
and the government shall be upon his shoulder:
and his name shall be called Wonderful, Counsellor,
The mighty God, The everlasting Father,
The Prince of Peace.

ISAIAH 9:6

*Kara* arranged the last package under the tree and glanced at the clock—1:15 A.M. She sighed. She felt physically exhausted, but her mind was still going a hundred miles a minute, and she knew she'd never be able to sleep. A cup of hot cocoa would be nice anyway. She might as well relax and enjoy the beauty of the tree for a few minutes. After all, it wouldn't be long before three excited children would be tearing into the perfection.

As she looked around, Kara's gaze came to rest on the papier-mâché nativity scene she had made when she and Luke had first married. It wasn't as fancy as some of the store-bought sets, and she sometimes thought her camels looked more like dinosaurs. Still, the set was special. She had thought of replacing it but always changed her mind when she thought of the pleasure her children received in arranging the figures and acting out the Christmas story.

Her mind went back a week and a half to when her family had decorated for the holiday season. She could still see Molly, her seven-year-old daughter as she placed Mary beside the manger and began to quietly sing a lullaby. Then Molly had repeated one of Kara's own bedtime phrases. "Sleep peacefully little one."

*What could be more peaceful than a sleeping child?* wondered Kara. When she tucked her babies into bed, she always felt such a gentle peace herself. Did Mary feel that same sense of peace as she tucked her child and Lord into His hay-filled cradle? What had the prophet Isaiah said this child would be named? The Prince of Peace. Certainly Mary must have been overwhelmed with peace—the peace only her child could bring.

FOR CHRIST IS BORN OF MARY,
AND GATHERED ALL ABOVE,
WHILE MORTALS SLEEP, THE ANGELS
KEEP THEIR WATCH OF WONDERING LOVE.
O MORNING STARS TOGETHER,
PROCLAIM THE HOLY BIRTH,
AND PRAISES SING TO GOD THE KING,
AND PEACE TO MEN ON EARTH!

PHILLIPS BROOKS,
from "O Little Town of Bethlehem"

And she brought forth her firstborn son,
and wrapped him in swaddling clothes,
and laid him in a manger;
because there was no room for them in the inn.

LUKE 2:7

*The LORD will give strength unto his people;
the LORD will bless his people with peace.*

PSALM 29:11

I heard the bells on Christmas Day.
Their old familiar carols play.
And wild and sweet the words repeat
Of peace on earth goodwill to men.

HENRY WADSWORTH LONGFELLOW

# Silent Night

Silent night, holy night,
All is calm, all is bright
Round yon virgin mother and Child.
Holy Infant, so tender and mild,
Sleep in heavenly peace,
Sleep in heavenly peace.

Silent night, holy night,
Son of God, love's pure light;
Radiant beams from Thy holy face
With the dawn of redeeming grace,
Jesus, Lord, at Thy birth,
Jesus, Lord, at Thy birth.

Silent night, holy night
Wondrous star, lend thy light;
With the angels let us sing,
Alleluia to our King;
Christ the Savior is born,
Christ the Savior is born!

JOSEF MOHR

*First keep the peace within yourself,*
*then you can also bring*
*peace to others.*

THOMAS À KEMPIS

And when they had seen it, they made known abroad
the saying which was told them concerning this child.
And all they that heard it wondered
at those things which were told them by the shepherds.
But Mary kept all these things,
and pondered them in her heart.

LUKE 2:17–19

Time was with most of us, when Christmas Day encircling all our limited world like a magic ring, left nothing out for us to miss or seek; bound together all our home enjoyments, affections, and hopes; grouped everything and everyone round the Christmas fire, and made the little picture shining in our bright young eyes, complete.

CHARLES DICKENS

*The LORD lift up his countenance upon thee, and give thee peace.*

NUMBERS 6:26

# Incarnation of Peace

And the peace of God, which passeth all understanding,
shall keep your hearts and minds through Christ Jesus.

PHILIPPIANS 4:7

*Kara's* thoughts shifted to the tiny figure of a baby in the manger. One of her favorite Christmas carols, "Away in a Manger," came to mind as she considered whom this figure represented. *Away in a manger, indeed,* thought Kara. She'd grown up on a farm and had seen what these feed troughs went through. She knew that calves weren't the most well-mannered dinner companions one could ask for. And sweet as the hay smelled, she didn't think she'd care to tuck her newborn baby away in it—especially not if he were to be surrounded by hungry animals eagerly eying his mattress.

As Kara pondered this, she realized that Jesus, accustomed to all the glory of heaven, knew that these were the conditions He would be coming into. He knew His surroundings would be crude and that His first visitors would be a group of poor shepherds.

Kara realized, too, that Jesus knew all along He would face conditions far worse than those of the crude little Bethlehem stable. He knew from the beginning that He would hang on a cruel Roman cross and take upon Himself the sins of this wicked world.

*What a sweet peace,* Kara thought. *Jesus came willingly and peacefully into this sin-sick world, took my guilt upon Himself, and offers me that same sweet peace. How great His love is!*

AWAY IN A MANGER, NO CRIB FOR A BED,
THE LITTLE LORD JESUS
  LAID DOWN HIS SWEET HEAD.
THE STARS IN THE SKY
  LOOKED DOWN WHERE HE LAY
THE LITTLE LORD JESUS, ASLEEP ON THE HAY.

*Joy is like restless day;*
*peace divine like quiet night.*

ADELAIDE PROCTOR

*But thou, Bethlehem Ephratah, though thou be little among the thousands of*
*Judah, yet out of thee shall he come forth unto me that is to be ruler in*
*Israel; whose goings forth have been from of old, from everlasting.*

MICAH 5:2

*For peace of mind, we need to resign as*
*general manager of the universe.*

LARRY EISENBERG

# Voices in the Mist

The time draws near the birth of Christ:
The moon is hid; the night is still;
The Christmas bells from hill to hill
Answer each other in the mist.

Four voices of four hamlets round,
From far and near, on mead and moor,
Swell out and fail, as if a door
Were shut between me and the sound:

Each voice four changes on the wind,
That now dilate, and now decrease,
Peace and goodwill, goodwill and peace,
Peace and goodwill, to all mankind.

ALFRED LORD TENNYSON

Of the increase of his government and peace
there shall be no end, upon the throne of David,
and upon his kingdom, to order it,
and to establish it with judgment and
with justice from henceforth even for ever.
The zeal of the LORD of hosts will perform this.

ISAIAH 9:7

*When you find peace within
yourself, you become the kind of person
who can live at peace with others.*

PEACE PILGRIM

But when the fulness of the time was come, God sent forth his
Son, made of a woman, made under the law.

GALATIANS 4:4

*It is "My own peace I give you."*
*Not, NOTICE, the world's peace.*

RUMER GODDEN

And came and preached peace to you which were afar off,
and to them that were nigh.
For through him we both have access
by one Spirit unto the Father.

EPHESIANS 2:17–18

*And in His will is our peace.*

DANTE ALIGHIERI

# Behold the Lamb

Behold the Lamb of God,
which taketh away the sin of the world.

JOHN 1:29

*There* were two figures of shepherds near the stable. One was standing, staff in hand, the other was kneeling, a little lamb clutched in his grasp.

*Perhaps,* thought Kara, *the little lamb has become a pet to the young shepherd.* Kara remembered the sheep that her grandparents had kept on their little hobby farm. She had loved to watch the lambs bouncing around in the pasture. She thought back to the summer she had turned nine. There'd been a lamb that had lost its mama. Kara had promptly adopted the orphan and dubbed it "Snowflake." She'd helped to bottle-feed and otherwise care for her lamb, and she and Snowflake had been constant companions.

*But our sheep were pretty much just for fun,* Kara thought. *Once I claimed Snowflake as my own, I didn't have to give her up.*

Was that little shepherd clinging to his lamb in fear that he'd have to give him up for a Passover meal or burnt offering? After all, that's what his job was all about. Was he thinking of the angel's announcement, "Unto you is born this day in the city of David a Saviour, which is Christ the Lord"? Was he rejoicing in the peace that the angel had spoken of, knowing that even as he knelt there beside the manger, he was gazing at Jesus, God's perfect Lamb—the One who would be the ultimate sacrifice to pay the price for his sins?

*Maybe,* Kara reasoned, *just maybe the young shepherd realizes that the true peace he is searching for can be given to him by the tiny baby on a bed of hay.*

HARK! THE HERALD ANGELS SING

GLORY TO THE NEWBORN KING

PEACE ON EARTH, AND MERCY MILD,

GOD AND SINNERS RECONCILED!

CHARLES WESLEY

*Therefore being justified by faith,*
*we have peace with God*
*through our Lord Jesus Christ.*

ROMANS 5:1

"PEACE ON THE EARTH, GOOD WILL TO MEN,
FROM HEAVEN'S ALL GRACIOUS KING."
THE WORLD IN SOLEMN STILLNESS LAY,
TO HEAR THE ANGELS SING.

EDMUND HAMILTON SEARS, from "It Came Upon the Midnight Clear"

Now the *God of peace*, that brought again from the
dead our Lord Jesus, that great shepherd of the sheep,
through the blood of the everlasting covenant,
Make you perfect in every good work to do his will, working
in you that which is wellpleasing in his sight, through Jesus
Christ; to whom be glory for ever and ever. Amen.

HEBREWS 13:20–21

# While Shepherds Watched Their Flocks

While shepherds watched their flocks by night,
All seated on the ground,
The angel of the Lord came down,
And glory shone around,
"Fear not!" said he, for mighty dread
Had seized their troubled mind.
"Glad tidings of great joy I bring
To you and all mankind.
To you, in David's town, this day
Is born of David's line
A Savior, who is Christ the Lord,
And this shall be the sign,
The heavenly Babe you there shall find
To human view displayed,
All meanly wrapped in swathing bands,
And in a manger laid.
All glory be to God on high,
And to the Earth be peace;
Good will henceforth from heaven to men
Begin and never cease!"

NAHUM TATE

*Peace* was the first thing the angels sang.

*Peace* is the mark of the sons of God.

*Peace* is the nurse of love.

*Peace* is the mother of unity

*Peace* is the rest of blessed souls.

*Peace* is the dwelling place of eternity.

LEO THE GREAT

These things I have spoken unto you, that in me ye might
have peace. In the world ye shall have
tribulation: but be of good cheer;
I have overcome the world.

JOHN 16:33

*And* the angel said unto them, Fear not: for, behold, I bring you good tidings of great joy, which shall be to all people.

LUKE 2:10

*We shall find peace.*
*We shall hear the angels;*
*we shall see the sky,*
*sparkling with diamonds.*

ANTON CHEKHOV

*For* the mountains shall depart, and the hills be removed; but my kindness shall not depart from thee, neither shall the covenant of my peace be removed, saith the LORD that hath mercy on thee.

ISAIAH 54:10

# Journey to Peace

Where is he that is born King of the Jews?
for we have seen his star in the east,
and are come to worship him.

MATTHEW 2:2

*Three* men in elegant clothing and carrying finely carved boxes completed the scene. Kara's pastor had once mentioned that there had probably been quite a few more wise men than the three normally mentioned. She figured this trio was just representative of the number of precious gifts mentioned in Matthew.

*So how many wealthy, important men actually did leave their comfortable homes to follow an unusual star?* mused Kara. *Did they even know for sure what they were looking for?*

Kara recalled that the wise men had asked Herod where the King of the Jews was to be born. She wondered why they would be so interested in the King of the Jews. Did they go searching for all newborn babies who were heirs to thrones? As she continued to ponder this, she began to realize that these men knew the Scriptures. They knew that this baby was much more than an earthly king; He was the promised Messiah—the Savior of the world.

*That's why they could leave their comforts and follow a star to find a baby. God had fulfilled His promise to send the Messiah. Surely they could trust Him to lead them by His star.*

*Peace,* thought Kara. *These men had every earthly pleasure they could possibly desire. What they were searching for was a* true and lasting peace. They knew that would come only if they took the rough journey through the sand to find the King of the Jews—the only One capable of giving true and lasting peace.

*All men desire peace,
but few desire the things
that make for peace.*

THOMAS À KEMPIS

OBSERVE GOOD FAITH AND JUSTICE TOWARD ALL
NATIONS. CULTIVATE PEACE AND HARMONY WITH ALL.

GEORGE WASHINGTON

*And let the peace of God rule
in your hearts, to the which also ye are called
in one body; and be ye thankful.*

COLOSSIANS 3:15

I WANT ALL OF YOU TO TAKE ON WINGS AND
FLY SWIFTLY TO REPOSE IN THAT BLESSED PEACE POSSESSED
BY A SOUL THAT IS ALL FOR GOD.

FRANCES XAVIER CABRINI

# Christmas Everywhere

EVERYWHERE, everywhere, Christmas tonight!
Christmas in lands of the fir-tree and pine,
Christmas in lands of the palm-tree and vine,
Christmas where snow peaks stand solemn and white,
Christmas where cornfields stand sunny and bright.
Christmas where children are hopeful and gay,
Christmas where old men are patient and gray,
Christmas where peace, like a dove in his flight,
Broods o'er brave men in the thick of the fight;
Everywhere, everywhere, Christmas tonight!
For the Christ-child who comes is the Master of all;
No palace too great, no cottage too small.

PHILLIPS BROOKS

WHEN THEY SAW THE STAR, THEY
REJOICED WITH EXCEEDING GREAT JOY.

MATTHEW 2:10

*Peace is always beautiful.*

WALT WHITMAN

Now the Lord of peace himself give
you peace always by all means.
The Lord be with you all.

2 THESSALONIANS 3:16

*And* when they were come into the
house, they saw the young child with Mary
his mother, and fell down, and worshipped him: and
when they had opened their treasures,
they presented unto him gifts; gold, and
frankincense and myrrh.

MATTHEW 2:11

*God* rest ye, little children; let nothing you afright,
For Jesus Christ, your Savior, was born this happy night;
Along the hills of Galilee the white flocks sleeping lay,
When Christ, the child of Nazareth, was born on
Christmas day.

DINAH MULOCK CRAIK

# Depart in Peace

Lord, now lettest thou thy servant depart in peace,
according to thy word:
For mine eyes have seen thy salvation,
Which thou hast prepared
before the face of all people;
A light to lighten the Gentiles,
and the glory of thy people Israel.

LUKE 2:29–32

As Kara finished contemplating the holy scene before her, her thoughts shifted to a beautiful but often overlooked part of the Christmas story. In her mind she saw an old gentleman in Jerusalem who made regular treks to the temple to worship. She knew little about Simeon other than that he'd been promised by the Holy Spirit that he would not taste death before seeing the promised Messiah.

*Of all of the thousands upon thousands of people waiting for Messiah, why would God have chosen to make this promise to Simeon?* wondered Kara. *He must have had a deep and very personal relationship with his heavenly Father.*

Kara pulled her Bible from the coffee table in front of her and turned to the portion of Luke that contained this story. As she began reading, she thought of the great joy Simeon must have felt that day as he hurried to do the bidding of the Holy Spirit. She could almost feel the warmth of the smile on his wrinkled face as he pulled the child close and blessed the Lord.

"Lord, now lettest thou thy servant depart in peace." Kara whispered the words. Again she thought of the relationship Simeon must have had with God.

*He was ready to die—even looking forward to it,* thought Kara. *His great desire and only real need was to see the Lord's salvation. Once that happened he was ready to meet God face-to-face.*

The reality of the story made Kara's heart beat a little faster as she realized how like Simeon everyone is. *All we need is to see and accept the salvation of the Lord. Then we, too, can say "Lettest thou thy servant depart in peace." What an awesome gift!*

*Peace is. . .understanding the "oneness" of God and the "oneness" with God.*

AUTHOR UNKNOWN

*I will both lay me down in peace, and sleep: for thou, LORD, only makest me dwell in safety.*

PSALM 4:8

Christmas is not a time nor a season,
but a state of mind.
To cherish peace and goodwill,
to be plenteous in mercy,
is to have the real spirit of Christmas.

CALVIN COOLIDGE

*Mercy unto you, and peace, and love, be multiplied.*

JUDE 2

# Beautiful Christmas

O'er the hills and adown the snowy dells,
As the echoes ring of the Christmas bells,
Angel songs in our hearts resound again,
Singing peace on earth and good will to men!

Bring good will to the suffering and sad;
Speak the tender word that shall make them glad;
Tell them how, o'er the hills of Bethlehem
When the angels sang, 'twas good news for them.
Peace on earth! bid all strife and tumult cease;
For this night again gives the Lord His peace;
While our hands shall His temple beautify,
Carol, glory be unto God most high.

So glad hearts on this happy Christmas night
Bring your gifts of love, make His altar bright;
Sing glad songs that shall sweetly sound as when
Angels sang of peace and good will to men.

MARY B. SLADE

*Peace is the deliberate adjustment of my life to the will of God.*

AUTHOR UNKNOWN

THOU WILT KEEP HIM IN PERFECT PEACE,
WHOSE MIND IS STAYED ON THEE: BECAUSE HE
TRUSTETH IN THEE.

ISAIAH 26:3

*Let us have peace.*

ULYSSES S. GRANT

*G*race and peace be multiplied unto you through the knowledge of God, and of Jesus our Lord.

2 PETER 1:2

---

*Peace* is normally a great good, and normally coincides with righteousness, but it is righteousness and not peace which should bind the conscience of a nation as it should bind the conscience of an individual; and neither a nation nor an individual can surrender conscience to another's keeping.

THEODORE ROOSEVELT

*In* the midst of all the hustle, bustle, and excitement of this holiday season, take time to pause and reflect upon the most precious gift of all—the gift of God's Son. Through Him you can know true and lasting peace—the kind only He can give. It is my prayer that you will be blessed with this abundant peace today and always.

*For* God so loved the world,
that he gave his only begotten Son, that whosoever believeth in him
should not perish, but have everlasting life.

JOHN 3:16

*Merry Christmas!*